Haggis: The Recipe Book
30 ways with haggis

First published in 2012
by
Aird Trading (publishing)
www.scotlandbooks.co.uk

Authors: Lynne Woods & Doug Vickers

ISBN 978-0-9562126-4-1

Introduction

Long since considered a staple part of the Scottish diet, Haggis has, in recent years, undergone a change of image. Eaten in celebratory style on Burns' Night for over two hundred years, for the rest of the year it has been largely considered a rather ordinary, if tasty, dish - served alongside the customary mashed potatoes and turnip. Happily, however, it is at long last being recognised for its versatility and that is what this collection of recipes sets out to explore. The unique taste and texture of haggis lend themselves to many culinary possibilities and combinations, not simply served "straight" but as a filling, an accompaniment or as seasoning to other ingredients. The recipes which follow use haggis imaginatively with ingredients which either complement its flavour or are themselves enhanced by the flavour of the haggis.

Whilst some cooks like to produce their own home-made version, there are many different high quality brands readily available – varying in texture from rough to smooth and in presentation from encased in a "skin" to ready sliced. Taste also varies between brands, not to mention the many hundreds of haggis, some more spicy than others, created by individual butchers. Where a particular characteristic is desirable in a recipe this has been mentioned in the ingredients list.

With regard to recipes which combine cheese with haggis, there are definitely a few "do's" and "don'ts". In our opinion, some cheeses are simply the wrong flavour or texture to blend harmoniously with haggis. We would therefore recommend that you read the section about cheeses on page 6.

Most recipe books list ingredients sufficient to serve four, or even six, people. Given that it is usually easier to double or triple ingredients than to half them, we have (unless otherwise stated) used quantities which will serve two people. Where small quantities of onion are required, spring onions or shallots are a useful substitute for half an onion. It is not practical to always supply exact conversions between metric and imperial measures, as many amounts do not have "sensible" equivalents. For the best results, use either one or the other but do not mix the two. In some recipes, the quantities of haggis may seem small – this is either because, when combined with the other ingredients, the dish is quite filling or because the haggis is being used as a flavouring rather than as the main ingredient. Many proprietary ones weigh 500g. As haggis freezes successfully any surplus need not be wasted.

And finally......

Space did not permit the addition of the following to each individual recipe: "Set aside a glass of your favourite tipple and sip whenever tempted."

Contents

The Noble Haggis

Most countries have a national dish; Hungarian Goulash, Spanish Paella, Pizza from Italy, French Pot au Feu and, of course, the American Hamburger. Britain enjoys a separate "national" dish for each part of the Kingdom: The famed Irish Stew and Welsh Cawl are similar but with the addition of bacon in the latter. England has two favourites – Roast Beef and Yorkshire Pudding and Fish and Chips. Nowhere, however, is a single meal more a part of the national heritage than in Scotland where haggis is revered and positively celebrated, especially on January 25th each year, the birthday of Robert (Robbie) Burns whose eighteenth century poem "To a Haggis" was instrumental in ensuring the Haggis' place in the hearts of the nation.

In spite of tales of small, furry, four or six legged creatures with some legs shorter than the others to enable them to run around hills without falling over, haggis is made from the meat of the sheep. Historically it consisted of the minced heart, liver and lungs, combined with onions, oatmeal, suet, seasoning and spices. The mix was then stuffed into the cleaned stomach of the sheep and boiled for several hours. Modern haggis is cooked in the manufacture so only requires heating though.

The origins of haggis have become lost in the mists of time. It is commonly supposed to have originated in Scotland but evidence suggests that the stomachs of wild animals were employed as ready-made cooking vessels by early man after he had learned to harness the power of fire and the Ancient Romans produced a dish similar to haggis as a cheap and easy way to feed their armies on the move. From the fourteenth century, drovers herding cattle to southern markets found haggis a convenient way to store, transport and then cook a hearty meal. Recipes for "hagese" and "haggus", using offal and herbs, have been found from the fifteenth and seventeenth centuries. It is thought that the name might have its origins in the Scandinavian "hugga" or "hag" meaning "chop" or "minced" and that haggis as we would recognise it came into being sometime after the Viking invasion of the ninth century and before their departure some six centuries later.

As with many national dishes, haggis owes much of its popularity to economic factors, using the cheaper offal (internal organs) of the beast rather than more sought after prime cuts from the carcass. In Scotland, the offal would often be given to the labourers after the landowner, or laird, had taken the best meat.

Modern palates prefer a synthetic skin similar to that used in sausages and at least one manufacturer produces canned haggis which enables people to enjoy the benefits of a product which does not have to be chilled and which can be transported and stored without the risk of deterioration. Another deviation from original recipes is that "better" cuts of meat than offal are used. The basic flavour, however, remains the same – a delicious, wholesome and unique dish. Whilst haggis is now produced on a large scale in Scotland, many individual butchers still make their own, often including a secret ingredient. The result is a vast range of delightful and subtle variations but all with the same basic hearty flavour, some more spicy than others. There are even vegetarian versions with pulses and vegetables substituted for meat.

Nowadays the number of ways to eat haggis is limited only by the imagination of chefs. One popular way is to stuff a chicken breast with haggis and wrap it in bacon before baking. Another favourite, although perhaps not the most healthiest of meals in these cholesterol conscious times, is to coat it in batter before deep frying! However, the traditional, and still the most common way, of serving this much loved dish is with "neeps" (boiled and mashed swede*[1]) and "tatties" (mashed potato). A whisky sauce often accompanies the meal, although purists may prefer to take their "tipple" neat – either in a glass or poured directly over the haggis!

*[1] a pink skinned, yellow fleshed turnip – not the smaller, white fleshed variety of turnip.

Burns' Night

Burns' Night is celebrated in style each year in Scotland on January 25th, a celebration not just of the great poet's birthday in 1759 but of the haggis itself, "Great chieftan o' the puddin' race".

Robert Burns (1759 – 1796) *[2]

A typical Burns' supper involves the haggis being paraded to the dining table to the accompaniment of a piper. With great ceremony, the dish is then addressed with the words of Burns himself, the tongue-in-cheek, mock heroic poem thought to have been penned by Burns in 1786 when invited to eat at a friend's house. (See page 32.) Loosely translated, the poem extols the virtues of the haggis as a hearty meal for Scots, making them manlier than non-Scots who eat fancier, less substantial food and are scorned as "feckles as wither'd rash" (as weak as a withered reed).

*[2] This image is in the public domain.

Haggis & Cheese - a harmonious combination.....

The idea of combining haggis with cheese would possibly make the toes of many Scots curl in horror. Indeed, some cheeses, especially strong flavoured, cheddar types, are far better left as the star attraction on a cracker or Scottish oatcake, or served in slabs alongside a crusty roll and some fruit chutney. However, milder and more subtle cheeses can complement and enhance the distinctive flavour of haggis in the most wonderful way.
Not surprisingly, some of the cheeses best suited for this are produced in Scotland which has many small creameries, between them producing a wide range of excellent cheeses. The unique flavour and texture of individual cheeses is determined by a host of factors: While pasteurised milk produces a more consistent product, cheese produced from raw milk has an earthiness and a much more natural taste. The flavour of cheese from cows which graze outside in the summer will differ during the winter months and depending on their feed. Cheeses also vary according to the length of time they are left to ripen or mature. Those which ripen from the outside to the centre can exhibit a marked difference between the inner part and that next to the rind.
In researching this book and testing the recipes, we invariably found that the best results were achieved from using tasty white cheeses which were neither overly strong in flavour nor too mild. Those with a definite "tangy" aftertaste proved ideal. Cheeses with a crumbly texture which go "blobby" rather than "stringy" when melted were our preferred choice, blending best with both the taste and texture of haggis.
Whilst the purists would decree that only Scottish cheese should be served with a Scottish dish, haggis is now enjoyed far beyond Scotland so we have listed below a selection of suitable cheeses from both north and south of the border. A brief description of the main qualities of each should enable cooks further afield to experiment and match with their own local cheeses.

Anster Cheese is hand made from the unpasteurised milk of home-bred Holstein Friesian cows at the St. Andrews Farmhouse Cheese Company near Anstruther on the Firth of Forth. It has a beautiful fresh flavour which is tangy but not overpowering. It crumbles beautifully and melts into delicious bobbles so its flavour remains distinct from that of the haggis, the two meeting the tongue in a harmonious partnership rather than a blended mass. Available by mail order. www.standrewscheese.co.uk Tel: 01333 312580.
Cromal, from the award winning Connage Highland Dairy, has a slightly "zingier" flavour but, again, goes superbly with haggis and crumbles well. It is an organic cheese produced on a family run farm at Ardersier on the shores of the Moray Firth and where, for much of the year, the cows graze in clover pastures. The most comparable non-Scottish cheese is Caerphilly which, although milder than Cromal, has much the same qualities. Online shop: www.connage.co uk Tel: 01667 462000

Cambus o' May also worked well. This is the signature cheese of the Cambus o' May Cheese Company on Royal Deeside. Slightly stronger in flavour than the other Scottish cheeses we used, it is fairly hard, hand-made from the curd of two separate days' unpasteurised milk, which gives it a marbled appearance. It is quite creamy in texture so it may be necessary to very finely chop it if it proves reluctant to crumble. Online shop: www.cambusomay.com Tel: 01339 753113 (We deliberately chose not to grate cheese so that it did not melt away and lose its distinctive flavour and texture amongst the other ingredients.)

South of the border and with very similar qualities to Anster Cheese, **Mrs. Kirkham's Crumbly Lancashire** is produced on Beesley Farm at Goosnargh, near Preston. It is made the traditional way from unpasteurised cows' milk, cloth bound and sealed with butter. It has a fine crumbly texture and a delicious lemony aftertaste. To order visit their online shop at www.mrskirkhams.com or telephone 01772 865335.

Another suitable alternative to the Scottish cheeses, again from the north west of England, is **Grandma Singleton's Crumbly Lancashire.** Not as dry as a Wensleydale cheese, it is produced by fourth generation family cheesemakers. It is made with pasteurised cows' milk and has an acidity and slight saltiness which once again provides a delightful sharpness of flavour. Its texture, similar to the Anster, is ideal for crumbling or melting onto haggis. For details telephone 01772 782112 or visit www.grandma-singletons.co.uk

For anyone who cannot obtain the above cheeses, **Wensleydale** is more or less universally available but only that made at Hawes in North Yorkshire is the genuine Dales cheese. (This can be distinguished by the Wensleydale crest which features a cow's head symbol.) Although slightly more strongly flavoured than Anster and with an "all through" tang rather than an "after-tang", it provides a good substitute and crumbles well.

We also tried Cheshire cheese. While this crumbled conveniently, we found the flavour just a little too mild and consequently overpowered by that of the haggis. Cooking "is a matter of taste" – while we hope you will try our recommendations, do not be afraid to experiment.

Traditional "Haggis, Neeps & Tatties" with Whisky Sauce

Ingredients: (Serves two)
1 small or medium haggis
1 small swede
Or 1/2 swede & 2 carrots
2 large potatoes suitable for mashing
Salt, black pepper & sugar to season
Butter (optional)
oatcakes to serve, two per person

For the sauce:
6 tablespoons single cream
4 teaspoons whisky
1/2 teaspoon Dijon mustard
1/2 teaspoon brown sugar

To cook:

1. Boil, steam or microwave the haggis according to the instructions. Peel & dice the swede (and carrots if using). Boil with some salt, black pepper and 1/4 teaspoon sugar for 10 - 15 minutes until tender. Peel, quarter and boil the potatoes for 10 - 15 minutes until cooked.

2. Drain & mash the swede/carrot (with a knob of butter if preferred). Drain & mash the potatoes (also with a knob of butter if required).

To make the sauce:

2. Gently heat all the ingredients together in a saucepan or microwave. Do not allow to boil.

To serve:

3. Use the point of a sharp knife to cut the oatcakes in half. Use an egg ring or pastry cutter to form the haggis, neeps and tatties into circles (see picture). Decorate with the oatcakes. Either drizzle the sauce over or serve separately in a jug.

This is the traditional way to eat Haggis on Burns' Night (January 25th) to celebrate the birthday of the Scottish bard."Neeps" are swedes (or turnips). "Tatties" are potatoes!

Notes: A true Scot might well dispense with the cream, mustard, sugar & saucepan & simply pour the neat whisky over the haggis!
Why not cook double quantities & reserve half for haggis burgers? (page 9)

"Haggis, Neeps & Tattie" Burgers with Lemon Whisky Sauce & Crispy Onion Rings

Ingredients: (Serves two)

For the burgers: roughly equal quantities of fresh or leftover haggis, mashed swede & mashed potato (see page 8) 200g/7 oz. of each makes four burgers.

75g/3 oz. flour

additional flour for shaping

For the onion rings:

1 medium onion cut into 1cm. slices

Approx. 75g/3 oz. flour

2 egg whites

Oil for frying

For the sauce:

50g/2 oz. butter or margarine

2 egg yolks

5 teaspoons lemon juice

2.5 teaspoons whisky

1/2 teaspoon sugar

300ml/10.5 fl. oz. single cream

A great way to use leftover haggis, neeps & tatties! (See page 8)

To prepare the burgers:

1. Combine the haggis, swede & potato with 75g/3 oz. flour. On a floured board, divide and shape into four burgers. (Tip: If the haggis is too crumbly warm it slightly.) Set aside in the fridge to firm.

To prepare the onion rings:

2. Push out the centres of the onion slices to form rings. Beat the egg whites until just beginning to turn frothy. Put 75g/3 oz. of flour on a plate. Dip each onion ring into the flour, then the egg white, then the flour again. Set aside.

To make the sauce:

3. Melt the butter or margarine until foaming but not browning. Beat together the egg yolks, lemon juice & whisky. Add the melted butter, sugar & 3 tablespoons of hot water. Stir in the cream. Heat gently, stirring continuously until thickened. Do not allow to boil. Add more lemon juice or whisky to taste if required. Set aside. C'td.....

"Haggis, Neeps & Tattie" Burgers (C'td)

To cook the burgers:

4. Fry the burgers for about 10 minutes each side until well heated through and crispy and browning on the outside.

To cook the onion rings:

5. Heat 1/2 cm. depth of oil until hot enough to make the onion rings sizzle when added to the pan. Fry for 3 - 4 minutes each side until cooked and golden. Drain on kitchen paper and keep warm.

To serve:

6. Gently reheat the sauce, drain the haggis burgers on kitchen paper and serve alongside the onion rings with the sauce either drizzled over or served separately.

Notes:

The burgers are quite filling so are perhaps better served with a salad rather than on a bun!

Haggis and Ham Rolls

Ingredients: (Serves two)

75g/3oz. haggis finely chopped

200g/7 oz. puff pastry thawed

75g/3 oz. cooked ham finely chopped

2 oatcakes crumbled

Just over 25ml/1 fl.oz. milk

beaten egg to glaze

To make:

1. Pre-heat the oven to 200'C/400'F/Gas 6. Combine the haggis, ham, oatcakes & milk to a stiff consistency.

2. Roll the pastry thinly & trim to a rectangle. Spread the filling over, leaving a 1cm. border and roll up. With the seams on the underside, cut into six. Decorate with the trimmings shaped into leaves or mini haggis shapes. Glaze with the beaten egg and bake on a lined baking tray for 15 - 20 minutes until golden.

Delicious hot or cold!

Haggis, leek and Ham Pie

Ingredients: (Serves two)
150g/5 oz. haggis diced
225g/8 oz. puff pastry thawed
1 medium leek sliced
1 stick celery sliced
5 button mushrooms sliced
1 tablespoon cornflour
50ml/2 fl. oz. milk
110g/4 oz. cooked ham diced
Beaten egg to glaze

To make:

1. Pre-heat the oven to 220'C/ 425'F/ Gas 7.
2. Simmer the leek & celery for 5 minutes in just enough water to cover. Add the mushrooms & continue cooking until the leek is tender.
3. Mix the cornflour and milk to a smooth paste & add to the pan, along with the ham. Bring back to the boil until the sauce thickens then reduce the heat and add the haggis. Season to taste. Transfer the mixture to two individual pie dishes.
4. Roll out the pastry and cover each dish, using the trimmings to decorate with haggis shapes or leaves. Glaze with beaten egg and bake for 15 - 20 minutes until the pastry is cooked and golden.

This is a filling pie so why not serve simply with some green vegetables? (It is also extremely tasty served cold with a salad or in a picnic.)

Haggis, Walnut & Cheese Topper for Fish

Ingredients: (serves two)
2 pieces of white, boneless fish
For the topper:
125g/4.5 oz haggis finely chopped
75g/3 oz tangy white cheese crumbled (see page 6-7)
12 walnut halves crushed
a small knob butter or margarine

To make the topping:

1. Melt the butter or margarine in a saucepan. Add the haggis, cheese & walnuts. Warm gently to combine, taking care not to let the cheese become stringy. Set aside.

To complete:

2. Grill, poach or microwave the fish.

3. Gently reheat the haggis mixture and pile on top of the fish. Garnish with lemon and serve at once.

Serving suggestion:
Serve with chips, peas and tomato. Garnish with lemon

Crispy Haggis & Bacon Roll-Ups

Ingredients: (Servees two)
75g/3 oz. haggis sliced very thinly
4 large thin slices of bread
8 rashers lean, rindless bacon
You will need:
A rolling pin & 8 cocktail sticks

Method: 1. Pre-heat the oven to 200'C/400f/Gas 6).

2. Remove the crusts and roll out the bread slices to flatten. On each, lay two rashers of bacon with the haggis on top. Roll up, securing with cocktail sticks. Line a baking tin with baking parchment and bake for approximately 25 minutes until crisp and golden, turning half way through.

Haggis & Tomato Pasta Bake

Ingredients: (Serves two)
250g/9oz haggis thinly sliced
150g/5 oz. dried pasta
1 small onion peeled & Chopped
1 clove garlic crushed
1 stick celery diced
1small courgette diced
1 x 400g tin chopped tomatoes
1 teaspoon mixed dried herbs
110g/4 oz. white, tangy cheese
Oil for frying

To make:

1. Turn the oven to 200'C/400'f/gas 6.
2. Cook the pasta according to the instructions on the packet. Drain & set aside.
3. Heat the oil in a saucepan & fry the onion, garlic, courgette, celery & herbs gently for 3 minutes before adding the tomatoes and their juice. Simmer gently for a further five minutes, remove from the heat & add the drained pasta.
4. Tip half of the mixture into a greased, ovenproof dish. Lay the Haggis on top (remove the skins first if necessary) then cover with the remaining pasta mix. Crumble the cheese over the top and bake for approx. 20 minutes until the cheese is melting into "blobs" - slightly longer if you prefer it bubbling and golden.

Serving suggestions: Serve with baked beans or a crispy salad.

Haggis & Beetroot Flan

Ingredients: (Serves two)
200g/7oz. haggis finely chopped
125g/4.5 oz. puff pastry thawed
2 tablespoons chutney or pickle
110g/4 oz. cooked beetroot (not pickled)
beaten egg to glaze

Haggis & Beetroot Flan (C'td)

To make:

1. Pre-heat the oven to 200'C/400'F/Gas 6.

2. Roll out the pastry thinly to a rectangle & trim the edges to neaten. Without cutting through the pastry, score a 1cm border all round. Brush the border with beaten egg. Keeping within the border, spread the chutney or pickle over the pastry and cover with haggis. Using a kitchen glove (or plastic bag over your hand), coarsely grate the beetroot and pile on top of the haggis.

4. Bake on a lined baking tin for approx. 25 minutes until the pastry is golden and has risen around the edge of the tart.

Notes:
The plum chutney on page 15 gives a good flavour to this dish.

Cheesy Haggis, Bacon & Mushroom Puffs

Ingredients: (serves two)

75g/3 oz. haggis, chopped

One pre rolled sheet or 1/2 block puff pastry thawed

75g/3 oz. tangy white cheese

2 rashers lean, unsmoked bacon

4 button mushrooms

beaten egg or milk to glaze

To prepare: 1. Turn the oven to 200'C/ 400'f/ gas 6.

2. Cut/roll the pastry into four rectangles, each approx. 13cm x 10cm (5" x 4") On each, score a 1cm (1/2") border without cutting right through the pastry. Place on a lined baking tray, leaving space between them. Working within the scored borders, cover each with the crumbled cheese, then haggis. Arrange strips of bacon over the haggis, as in the picture, then finally the sliced mushrooms. Glaze the borders with egg or milk.

3. Bake for 20 - 25 minutes until cooked & golden.

Served cold, these make an interesting addition to a picnic, or miniature ones are attractive served as part of a cold buffet.

Oaty Haggis Rissoles with Plum Chutney

Ingredients: (Serves two)
4 slices haggis (skin off)
1 egg beaten
1 tablespoon flour
75g/3 oz. pinhead oatmeal
Oil for frying

For the chutney:
2 large, firm plums
4 tablespoons of malt vinegar
2 tablespoons brown sugar
2 teaspoons clear honey
50ml/2 fluid oz. water
2 teaspoons cornflour

The tartness of the chutney complements the flavour of the haggis. Ordinary oatmeal also works well.

To prepare: 1. Cover the plums with boiling water and set side.

To make the rissoles:

2.Put the beaten egg in a shallow dish and the flour and oatmeal on two separate plates. Dip each haggis slice into the flour, then egg, then oatmeal to coat completely. Place in the fridge to firm up.

To make the chutney:

3. Gently heat together the vinegar, brown sugar, honey and water. Remove the plums from the hot water. Use a sharp knife to remove the skins then chop into 1cm (1/2 inch) pieces. Add to the pan. Simmer gently until the plums are soft but not mushy. Remove from the pan and set aside. Boil the liquid rapidly for 2 minutes to reduce. Mix the cornflour with water to make a thin paste, add to the pan and stir until thickened. Return the plums to the mixture and allow to cool.

To cook the rissoles:

4.Heat the oil in a frying pan until sizzling hot. Fry the rissoles for 3 minutes each side until golden and crispy. Drain on kitchen paper.

Serving suggestion: Serve on a bed of wilted spinach alongside the chutney. Served cold, the rissoles also make a nice change for a picnic. This dish ,suprisingly, goes well with a sweet dessert wine such as Sauternes or Monbazillac.

Haggis & Mushroom Balls with Pasta & Herby Tomato sauce

Ingredients: (serves two)
400g/14 oz. haggis , skin off
1 small onion finely chopped
margarine
3 - 4 mushrooms finely chopped
1 egg beaten
5 tablespoons flour
oil for frying
spaghetti or other pasta

For the tomato sauce:
1 small onion finely chopped
1 level teaspoon dried mixed herbs
1 x 200g tin chopped tomatoes
black pepper

To make the Haggis Balls:

1. Cook the onion with a blob of margarine for 1 -2 minutes. Add the mushrooms & cook for a further 5 minutes. Add the roughly chopped haggis with 1 tablespoon of flour & cook for a further minute. Remove from the heat and leave until cool enough to handle.

2. Put 2 tablespoons of flour on a plate. Form the haggis mixture into walnut-sized balls & roll each in the flour. Place in the fridge to firm.

To make the sauce:

3. Cook the onion & herbs in margarine for 5 - 7 minutes until soft. Add the tomatoes & cook briskly for 4 - 5 minutes until the liquid is reduced. Season with black pepper to taste.

To cook:

4. Cook the pasta according to the instructions on the packet. Meanwhile, put the egg in a shallow dish and the remaining flour in another. Roll each haggis ball in egg then flour and fry in oil for 7 - 8 minutes, turning until they are cooked through and golden brown. Drain on kitchen paper.

5. Re-heat the sauce, drain the pasta and serve.

Notes: Make sure the oil is hot enough to seal the egg and flour coating.

Haggis and Carrot Flan

Ingredients: (Serves two)
110g/4oz haggis crumbled
175g/6 oz. shortcrust pastry
5 tablespoons marmalade
1 medium egg beaten with 1 tablespoon double cream
1 med. carrot coarsely grated
2 oatcakes crumbled

Method

1. Pre-heat the oven to 180'C/350'F/gas 4.
2. Grease a small, shallow flan dish. Line with the rolled out pastry.
3. Spread half the marmalade over the pastry. (Warm the marmalade to soften if necessary.) Use a little of the egg and cream mix to brush round the top edge of the flan case.
4. In a bowl, combine the haggis, carrot, remaining marmalade, egg oatcakes & cream to make a stiff paste. Spread over the pastry base. Bake at 180'C/350'F/gas 4for 15 mins. until set and beginning to brown then increase the heat to 200'c/400'f/gas 6 and cook for a further 10 - 15 minutes until golden brown.

Haggis and Bacon Rice Cakes

Ingredients: (Serves two)
110g/4 oz. haggis chopped
6 spring onions finely sliced
75g/ 3 oz. cooked long grain rice
4 rashers cooked lean chopped bacon

To make:

1. Pre-heat the oven to 190'C/375'F/Gas 5. 2.Combine all the ingredients. 3. Grease the inside of a 9cm. /3.5" pastry cutter. Place on a lined baking sheet. Fill the mould with the mixture, press down firmly and then gently ease the mould away. Repeat with the remaining mixture. 4. Bake at 190'C/375'F/gas 5 for 20 - 25 mins. until golden.

Haggis "Bolognese" with Egg Noodles

Ingredients: (serves two)
400g/14 oz. haggis, skin off
1 medium onion chopped
1/2 teaspoon dried mixed herbs
200g/7 oz. mushrooms chopped
oil for frying
1 x 400g tin chopped tomatoes
75g/3 oz. crumbly white cheese
egg noodles

To make:

1. Gently fry the onions & herbs together for 2 - 3 minutes. Add the mushrooms & cook for a further 5 minutes. Add the tomatoes, along with a splash of water. Cook for a further two minutes. Add the roughly chopped haggis. Reduce the heat & leave to warm through.
2. Cook the egg noodles according to the instructions on the packet.

To serve:

3. Drain the noodles, cover with the haggis mixture & top with crumbled cheese.

Haggis & Pork Loaf

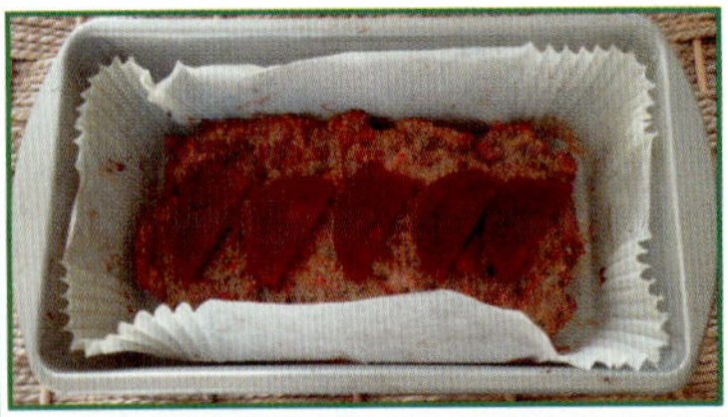

Delicious hot or cold!

Ingredients: (serves two)
200g/7 oz. haggis, skin off
6 chunky pork sausages skinned
6 rashers lean, rindless bacon chopped
100g/3.5 oz. fresh breadcrumbs
Cooked beetroot (not pickled) to garnish
You will need: A loaf tin, baking paper

To make:

1. Turn the oven to 190'C/375'F/Gas 5. Grease & line a small loaf tin.
2. Combine the haggis, sausagemeat, bacon & breadcrumbs in a food processor or with a fork. Press into the loaf tin. Bake for approx. 40 - 50 minutes until set & golden. Garnish with sliced beetroot.

Haggis & Beetroot lasagne

Ingredients: (Serves two)
300g/11oz. haggis chopped
300ml/10.5 fl. oz crème fraiche
1 teaspoon Dijon mustard
150g/5 oz. tangy white cheese
1 small onion chopped
4 medium mushrooms sliced
125g/4.5 oz. cooked beetroot (not pickled)
3 lasagne pasta sheets
oil for frying

To make:

1. Pre-heat the oven to 180'C/ 350'F/ gas 4.
2. Combine the crème fraiche, mustard and half of the tangy cheese. Warm gently in a saucepan or microwave to form a smooth sauce. (Do not allow to boil.) Set aside.

5. Fry the onion and mushroom together briskly for 2 -3 minutes until brown then reduce the heat & cook for a further 5 minutes. Dry the beetroot on kitchen paper and then, using a kitchen glove (or plastic bag over your hand), grate it coarsely. Add to the pan, along with the haggis and stir to warm through.
6. Pile the haggis mixture into an ovenproof dish & spread with half the cheese sauce. Arrange the roughly broken pasta sheets on top and then cover with the remaining sauce. Finally, scatter the remaining cheese over and bake for approx. 35 minutes until bubbling and golden.

Note: Overheating the crème fraiche will cause it to curdle. For an extra cheesy topping finish with 25g/1 oz. grated parmesan mixed with the crumbled tangy cheese!

Haggis Scotch Eggs

Ingredients: (serves two)
250g/9oz haggis chopped
4 hard boiled eggs cooled
250g/9oz sausage meat (see note)
Small pinch of mixed herbs
Either 2 Weetabix crumbled or 3 tablespoons of stuffing mix
3 tablespoons flour for rolling
To serve: small bag of salad leaves

> This is a bit fiddly to prepare but the results are well worth the effort! A great idea for picnics or packed lunches - make the day before.
> For a special buffet, make mini versions using quails' eggs.

Method

1. Pre-heat the oven to 190'C/375'F/gas 5.
2. Mix together the haggis, sausage meat and herbs (either with a fork or in a food processor).
3. Put the weetabix or stuffing mix onto a plate.
4. Shell the eggs.
5. On a floured board, divide the mixture into four. Roll or press each into a round large enough to wrap around an egg. (Use plenty of flour if the mix is too sticky.) Wrap each egg and roll on the plate of weetabix or stuffing mix to completely coat.
6. Transfer the scotch eggs to a lined baking sheet. Bake for between 20 and 30 minutes, turning several times, until the outside is brown and crispy. Drain on kitchen roll to remove any excess fat. Leave to cool.

> Notes:
> 5 chunky sausages split & "peeled" are less messy than sausage meat.
> Baking instead of deep frying scotch eggs is easier, safer & healthier.

Haggis Stuffed Leeks in a Tangy Cheese Sauce

Ingredients: (serves two)
125g/4.5 oz. haggis, skin off & cut into fingers
6 large leeks
½ teaspoon of Dijon mustard

For the cheese sauce:
75g/3 oz crumbly/tangy white cheese
1 x 320g tub crème fraiche

This dish is a little fiddly to prepare but the combination of flavours is yummy !

To prepare:

1. Pre-heat the oven to 190'C/375'f /gas 5.
2. Wash and trim the leeks. Cut 13 cm/5" from the white end of each. (See note below.) Simmer in salted water for 5 minutes to soften. Drain and refresh in cold water.

To make the sauce:

1. In a microwave or saucepan, warm together the crème fraiche, mustard and crumbled cheese. (Will curdle if overheated.)

To assemble:

1. Either use the end of a wooden spoon to gently push out the middles of the leeks, leaving four of the layers to form a tube (don't worry if it collapses at this stage) or cut lengthways half way through each leak and remove the middles to leave a rectangle four layers thick.
2. Stuff the leeks with the haggis fingers - either by pushing into the leek tubes or by rolling up in the leek rectangles. Arrange side by side in a greased ovenproof dish, pour over the sauce and bake for 20 - 25 minutes until bubbling & golden.

Notes: Low fat crème fraiche works well as it is runnier when heated. The remaining sections of leek may be cooked & served separately or used in Haggis and Barley Broth .(page 22)

Haggis & Barley Broth

Ingredients: (Serves two)
150g/5oz. haggis, skin off & diced
1 litre/2 pints vegetable stock (see notes)
50g/2oz. pearl barley
1 medium onion peeled & chopped
1 medium carrot sliced
1 medium leek sliced
1 stick of celery sliced (save the leaves)
A handful of chopped fresh herbs
Or ½ teaspoon of mixed dried herbs

Extra hungry? Serve with chunks of wholemeal bread.

For the dumplings:
50g/2 oz self raising flour
A large pinch of salt
25g/1 oz. suet
3 ½ tablespoons of cold water

Method

1. Simmer the barley in the stock for 15 minutes. Add the onion and carrot. Simmer for a further 10 mins.
2. To make the dumplings: Mix the flour, salt and suet. Add enough water to form a stiff dough. Divide into four and, on a floured plate, shape into balls. (These will double in size as they cook.)
3. Add to the broth the leeks, celery (not the leaves) and dried herbs if used. Gently place the dumplings on top. Cover and simmer for 25 minutes, turning the dumplings half way through.
4. When cooked, remove the dumplings from the pan, add the haggis and fresh herbs if used. Warm through then return the dumplings to the pan for 5 minutes to re-heat. Garnish with the celery leaves.

Notes:
Unlike meat stock, vegetable stock will not overpower the other flavours, especially the barley which absorbs the liquid as it cooks. There is no need to add seasoning – the haggis provides this.

Haggis Stuffed Chicken Breasts

Ingredients: (serves two)
150g/5 oz. haggis chopped
2 chicken breasts
4 - 6 rashers rindless, lean bacon

To make:

1. Pre-heat the oven to 200'C/400'F/Gas6
2. Using a sharp knife, cut a slit lengthways in the side of each chicken breast, leaving 1cm at each end uncut to form a pocket.
3. Stuff each chicken breast with haggis then wrap in two or three rashers of bacon, ensuring the ends are on the underside.
4. Bake for 25 - 35 minutes until the chicken is thoroughly cooked.

Serving suggestion:
As this dish is quite filling, simply serve with a selction of vegetables.

Haggis and Egg Nests

Ingredients: (Serves two)
25g/1oz haggis chopped
4 slices (thin) white bread
butter (or spread)
3 medium eggs beaten
black pepper
You will need: a deep bun tin

To make::

1. Turn the oven to 190'C/375'F/gas 5.
2. For the nests: Remove the crusts from the bread. Use a rolling pin to flatten each slice. Butter one side of each slice then push gently into the bun tin, butter side down. Trim the edges to neaten if necessary.

3. For the filling: Divide the haggis between the four nests. Beat the eggs with a little black pepper and pour over the haggis.
4. Bake for 15 - 20 minutes until the egg is set and the nest is crispy and golden.

Serve with baked beans for a healthy and popular children's meal or include as an unusual & tasty picnic treat.

Haggis Stuffed Peppers

Ingredients: (serves two)
125g/4.5 oz. haggis , skin off
2 medium red or yellow peppers
2 spring onions sliced into rings
150g/5 oz. bean sprouts rinsed
25g/1 oz mild, tangy cheese
oil for frying

To prepare:

1. Pre-heat oven to 200'C/400'F/Gas 6 (If pre baking peppers as below heat to 180'C/350'F/Gas4). Slice the top off the peppers and a sliver from the bottom so they will stand up. (Take care not to make a hole in the bottom!) Remove the white parts and seeds.
2. Soften the peppers for approx. 5 minutes in a microwave or 10 minutes in the oven on a greased tray (see above).

To make:

3. Fry the onions for 2 - 3 minutes until beginning to soften. Add the beansprouts and fry briskly for a minute then add the chopped haggis. Cook for a further minute, stirring gently until all the ingredients are combined and heated through.
4. Grease the bottom of a flan dish. Divide the mixture between the softened peppers, crumble the cheese over the top and bake at 200'C/400'F/Gas 6 for 15 minutes until the cheese is bubbling and golden.

Serving suggestion:
Serve on a bed of green salad or wilted spinach.

Haggis & Potato Fritters with Dressed Cherry Tomatoes

Ingredients: (Serves two)

4 slices of haggis skin off

2- 3 medium potatoes

For the batter:

110g/4 oz. flour

1/2 a teaspoon salt

1 egg beaten

175ml/6 fl.oz milk

1 teaspoon cold water

oil for frying

For the dressed tomatoes:

Cherry tomatoes (about 16)

1/2 a tablespoon olive oil

2 tablespoons chopped fresh herbs

To dress the tomatoes:

1. Rinse & half the tomatoes. Scatter the herbs over, drizzle with olive oil and mix well.

To make the batter:

2. Mix the flour and salt in a basin then whisk in the egg, milk amd water to make a thick, smooth batter.

To make the rissoles:

3. Scrub the unpeeled potatoes. Cut into 8 slices, approx. 1cm thick. Sandwich each slice of haggis between two slices of potato. Heat the oil until sizzling hot. Dip each fritter into the batter, shake off any excess then place carefully into the hot oil. If completely immersed, cook for about 5 minutes until golden and crispy and the potato is cooked. If shallow frying, cook for 3 - 4 minutes each side. Drain on kitchen paper. Serve immediately with the dressed tomatoes.

Notes:

It is important that the oil is hot enough to seal the fritters straight away but remember to take care when working with hot oil.

Haggis, Cheese & Pineapple Brunch

Ingredients: (Serves two)
4 slices of haggis skin off
4 crumpets
175g/6 oz. block of tangy cheese
4 pineapple slices
salad to garnish

The combination of flavours in this quick snack is surprisingly "more-ish"! The savoury haggis bridges the gap between the tangy cheese and the sweetness of the pineapple.

To make:

1. Slice the cheese into four. Using a pastry cutter slightly smaller than the crumpets, cut four rounds from the cheese slices. Reserve the corners.
2. Grill or microwave the haggis (both sides) until hot.
3. Lightly toast the crumpets on each side then place a cheese round on each. Return to the grill until the cheese begins to melt.
4. Place the haggis slices on top of the cheese and then a pineapple ring on top of the haggis. Crumble the remaining cheese into the top of the pineapple.
5. Return the crumpets to the grill until the cheese is golden and bubbling.

Haggis and Onion Hash

Ingredients: (Serves two)
1 small haggis skin off, 1 large onion,
2 large potatoes, oil for frying

This incredibly simple & filling meal is deceptively tasty!

To make:

1. Peel & chop the onion. Fry for a few minutes until beginning to soften. Scrub & dice the unpeeled potatoes. Add to the pan and continue cooking for a further 10 - 15 minutes until cooked & beginning to brown.
2. Stir in the haggis, heat through and serve at once.

Serving suggestion: Serve with mushy or marrowfat peas.

Haggis & Parsnip with Potato Rosti

Ingredients: (Serves two)
150g/5oz. haggis finely chopped
2 medium potatoes peeled & quartered
1 medium parsnip peeled & diced
Knob of butter
1 medium onion
Oil for frying
salt & black pepper to season

This is an unusual combination but the two distinctive flavours of haggis and parsnip go together surprisingly well.

To make:

1. Cook the potatoes in salted water for about 10 minutes until cooked but still firm. Drain & plunge into cold water. Set aside.

2. Simmer the parsnips for 10 - 15 minutes until well cooked. Drain, mash with a knob of butter & combine with the haggis. Return to the pan & heat through.

3. To make the rosti: While the parsnip is cooking, peel & coarsely grate the onion. Fry gently in the oil until beginning to soften. Drain & coarsley grate the potato. Add to the onion, with a little salt and pepper to season & press into the pan. Turn up the heat and fry for about 5 minutes until the underside is crispy. Carefully turn the rosti over and cook the other side till brown.

Serving suggestions:

Serve the haggis and parsnip alongside the rosti. Add a splash of colour with baked beans, cooked or pickled beetroot, grilled or raw tomatoes or a brightly coloured salad.

Haggis "Stovies" with Bubbly Cheese & Tomatoes

Ingredients: (serves two)

For the "Stovies":

175g/6 oz. haggis, diced
2 large potatoes
1 large onion, sliced
150ml/5 fl.oz./1/4 pint gravy
(granules work well or a beef stock cube in hot water)
Oil for frying
Oatcakes to serve (optional)

For the Bubbly Cheese & Tomatoes:

3 large tomatoes roughly chopped
110g/4 oz. Brie- type cheese
3 tablespoons orange marmalade
1 tablespoon brown sugar

Stovies is a traditional Scottish recipe which uses up leftover beef from the Sunday roast and so is often eaten on a Monday. Many Scottish households include their own variations & additions but the basic recipe contains potatoes onion and pre-cooked meat, .

To make the stovies:

1. Pre-heat the oven to 190'C/375'f / Gas 5.
2. Scrub or peel the potatoes. Part boil (about 10 minutes) then drain and dice.
3. Sauté the onions gently in oil for 5 - 10 minutes to soften. Add the part-cooked potatoes and the gravy. Increase the heat and cook for approx. 5 - 10 minutes until the potatoes and onions are browning (stir in the brown bits!)

To make the bubbly cheese tomatoes:

4. Pre heat the grill. Place the tomatoes in a flameproof dish. Cover with the roughly chopped cheese and dot with blobs of marmalade. Sprinkle with sugar and grill for 5 - 10 minutes until golden and bubbling. Serve with oatcakes alongside the Haggis Stovies.

Haggis with Honey Vegetable Stir Fry

Ingredients: (Serves two)
4 slices cooked Haggis
1 bunch of spring onions
1 medium carrot
2 sticks of celery
8 baby sweetcorn
A small head of broccoli
1 small courgette
A 250g/9 oz bag of beansprouts
Oil for frying

You will need: a wok or deep frying pan

For the stir-fry sauce:
3 teaspoons sugar
1 teaspoon clear honey
1 tablespoon hot water
1 tablespoon soy sauce
1 teaspoon lemon juice

To prepare the stir fry-sauce:

1. Dissolve the sugar & honey in the hot water. Stir in the soy sauce & lemon juice. Set aside.

To make the stir-fry:

2. Rinse & trim the vegetables as follows: Slice the onions and sweetcorn, break the broccoli into small flourettes, rinse & drain the bean sprouts. Cut the remaining vegetables into match sticks.
3. Heat the oil & fry the onions for one minute before adding the carrot, celery, sweetcorn & broccoli. Cook for a further minute. Add the courgette. Cook for another minute then stir in the sauce.
4. Turn up the heat. When steam is rising through the vegetables, place the haggis carefully on top. Cover the pan. After a minute, gently turn the haggis over. When it is thoroughly heated through remove and keep warm.
5. Add the beansprouts to the pan, fry briskly for two minutes then tip the vegetables into a warmed dish. Serve with the haggis slices on top.

Notes: Microwave haggis slices are ideal for this recipe.
Golden syrup may be substituted for honey.

Haggis "Olives"

Ingredients: (Serves two)
110g/ 4 oz. haggis chopped
4 minute steaks
Butter or margarine
1 small onion finely chopped
2 medium mushrooms chopped
50g/2 oz. hazelnuts
50g/2 oz. fresh breadcrumbs
300ml/10.5 fl.oz/1/2 pint gravy
Oil for frying

You will need:
8 wooden cocktail sticks

To make:

1. Pre-heat the oven to 190'C/375'F/Gas 5. Melt a large knob of butter or margarine in a saucepan. Fry the onion for a minute to soften then add the mushrooms & fry briskly until beginning to brown. Reduce the heat, add the haggis, nuts & breadcrumbs. Mix thoroughly, adding a little more butter or margarine if the mixture is too dry. Season to taste. (See below.)

To stuff the "olives":

2. Lay out each steak in turn. Spoon a quarter of the filling onto each and roll up, securing each with two cocktail sticks through the middle (horizontally so you can turn them over later).

3. Heat the oil in a frying pan and fry the "olives" for two minutes each side to brown. Place in an ovenproof dish.

3. Warm the gravy, pour over the "olives" & bake for 20 minutes, turning half way through.

Serving suggestion:
Serve with mashed potatoes to mop up the gravy!

Notes:
Beef olives are normally stuffed with uncooked sausage meat or minced meat. As haggis is already cooked, the baking time is less than for traditional beef olives.
With many of the recipes in this book the haggis is sufficient seasoning in itself. However, in this recipe, the breadcrumbs absorb some of the spiciness of the haggis so you may wish to add a little salt and/or pepper to taste.

Haggis & Whisky Pancakes with SouredTomatoes

Ingredients: (Serves two)
450g/ 1lb. haggis skin off
approx. 20 cherry tomatoes
8 tablespoons crème fraiche
2 tablespoons whisky
2 teaspoons sugar
Oil for frying

For the batter:
50g/2 oz. flour
Pinch of Salt
1 egg beaten
125ml/4.5 fl.oz milk
2 tablespoons cold water

To prepare the tomatoes:

1. Halve the tomatoes, combine with 2 tablespoons of the crème fraiche. Set aside.

To To make the batter:

2. Mix the flour and salt in a basin then whisk in the egg, milk and water to make a thin, smooth batter.

To make the filling:

3. In a saucepan, combine the remaining crème fraiche & chopped haggis, Warming gently to soften the haggis. Stir in the whisky & sugar to taste. Heat through. Cover & keep warm.

To make the pancakes:

4. Have a warm plate ready. Heat a very small amount of oil in a small frying pan until the oil is hot enough to make the batter sizzle. Add 5 - 6 tablespoons of batter (just enough to cover the bottom of the pan) & cook on a high heat until the surface begins to bubble. Turn & cook the other side, remove to the warm prepared plate and keep warm. Quickly cook the remaining pancakes, oiling the pan each time.

5. Either cover half of each pancake with the filling and fold over or spread the filling over the pancake and roll up. Serve immediately with the soured tomatoes.

Note:
For the filling, try using whipped cream instead of crème fraiche.
Remember to take care when working with hot oil.

Address To A Haggis..... by Robert Burns

Fair fa' your honest, sonsie face,
Great chieftain o' the puddin'-race!
Aboon them a' ye tak your place,
Painch, tripe, or thairm:
Weel are ye worthy o' a grace
As lang's my arm.

The groaning trencher there ye fill,
Your hurdies like a distant hill,
Your pin wad help to mend a mill
In time o' need,
While thro' your pores the dews distil
Like amber bead.

His knife see rustic Labour dight,
An' cut you up wi' ready slight,
Trenching your gushing entrails bright,
Like ony ditch;
And then, O what a glorious sight,
Warm-reekin', rich!

Then, horn for horn, they stretch an' strive:
Deil tak the hindmost! on they drive,
Till a' their weel-swall'd kytes belyve
Are bent like drums;
Then auld Guidman, maist like to rive,
Bethankit! hums.

Is there that owre his French ragout
Or olio that wad staw a sow,
Or fricassee wad make her spew
Wi' perfect scunner,
Looks down wi' sneering, scornfu' view
On sic a dinner?

Poor devil! see him owre his trash,
As feckles as wither'd rash,
His spindle shank, a guid whip-lash;
His nieve a nit;
Thro' bloody flood or field to dash,
O how unfit!

But mark the Rustic, haggis-fed,
The trembling earth resounds his tread.
Clap in his walie nieve a blade,
He'll mak it whissle;
An' legs an' arms, an' heads will sned,
Like taps o' thrissle.

Ye Pow'rs, wha mak mankind your care,
And dish them out their bill o' fare,
Auld Scotland wants nae skinking ware
That jaups in luggies;
But, if ye wish her gratefu' prayer
Gie her a haggis!

Did you know?

The song "Auld Lang Syne", sung all over the world on New Year's Eve, is also attributed to Robert Burns.

The authors are grateful to all the people who tested the recipes in this book, especially Andy, Gina, Andrew, Natalie and Audrey. Thanks also to Lynne's Dad who uncomplainingly ate haggis in various guises for many consecutive meals during the creation of this recipe book.
We would also like to thank the cheesemakers mentioned in the book and Susan Grizedale at E. H. Booth (Carnforth), for sharing their extensive knowledge and expertise.